When Did I Know I Was Black?

Chris Haley

Cyberwit.net
HIG 45 Kaushambi Kunj, Kalindipuram
Allahabad - 211011 (U.P.) India
http://www.cyberwit.net
Tel: +(91) 9415091004
E-mail: info@cyberwit.net

Printed at Repro India Limited.

Dedicated to Dorothy "Mom" Gray.

You have supported, encouraged, and cheered me on from as long as I can remember. This dedication is a small measure of appreciation for what you've meant to me.

Illustrations - Alan Haley

Cover Design - Chris Haley

Back Cover Photo courtesy of - Jonn Paris Jo'le

Your name identifies you.

Society labels you.

Your actions set you apart.

The Author

Praise For *When Did I Know I Was Black?*

In this set of poetic renumerations, Chris Haley has expressed the very essence of what it means to have "Known Rivers". He expresses what it means to have been battered by many natural and man-made currents and treacherous depths. His visceral and honest expressions of the pain and agony one goes through as a result of man's inhumanity to man, based on race or skin color, are bone-chilling and brilliantly articulated; raw and rare truth-telling.

Jesse Buggs, well-known mentor and advisor to individuals and organizations in a wide-cross section of human endeavor.

I've known Chris for a decade and he's the most cerebral, soulful individual I've ever encountered. It's completely befitting that he would write this wonderful collection of thought-provoking stanzas for creative consumption. In these pages, you will find reflections of US written in a voice of hard and soft truths, but love nonetheless. His heart is all over this collection, and we are better for it.

V. Helena Hall, Host & Executive Producer, Writer's Haven Show

When Did I Know I Was BLACK is a magnum opus by Chris Haley that brilliantly reflects the power of the collective BLACK spirit, perseverance, and journey through our nation's imperfect history. It compels the reader, no matter the skin they're in, to explore their own notion of race and humanity.

~ Bill Haley, Co-Founder, The Inherited Roots Project

"In his follow-up to Fists and Rainbows, Chris Haley continues in the vein of modern contemporaries Rachel Long, Hannah Lowe, and Danez Smith, looking inward to memories and histories concerning race and sexuality that are felt as much as they are remembered. Standout poems Slap Happy, Pinocchio, and Free embody the fire that forces us into the streets of protest and the just-below-the-surface melancholy that makes us cry into our pillows at midnight."

Chris Barkley, Film Producer, Co-Host of the MAKE IT Podcast, and Board Member of NPR, The Nashville Film Festival, and Columbia State University

Contents

Red

For the blood we share,
For the blood we shed,
We swear to spill more
In honor of those who led
Until their death left nothing to be said.
No extra infusions of love
Will we need
When we agree
We all bleed equally.

Black

We must be one.
Devotees of King,
Devotees of Malcolm,
We must be one.
If we are one,
A battle can be won.
If we are one,
A union can not be undone.
If we are one,
We are indivisible,
With liberty and justice in hand.
We rise as one together,
No longer allowing bigotry
To draw lines in the sand.
As one people,
As one nation,
As one miraculously rebuilt creation,
We will be strong.
We will hold onto
What is culturally ours
And securely share a transcendent Pride
Like our superpower.
With a clean conscience,
Our burden will be done.
We will be many,
But we will also be one.

Green

This world is so wide,
Its vistas so huge,
Why do we allow prejudice
To spoil amenable views?
Bigotry and bias perpetuate,
"I'm better than him."
"He's better than you."
What came first,
Classism or Racism?
Only a person who's
Covered with greenbacks,
Stifles a bigot's purview.

Free

I woke up with the weight of the world.
I was feeling weak, powerless,
Empty. My heart began racing out of futility.
So I watched some spoken word poetry to break my building
anxiety.
I know I'm an OG, but it lifted me.
And I tapped out to my iPhone keys.

I am inspired to admire
Words which spill out of me,
Because that's all I can see as a way
To address
Why you hate me.
A black man who is gay and loves history
And is born part of a heralded African
American legacy.
The root of it, you see,
is that I have always fought for those
Who lay at the bottom rung of society.
Even in love, it seems, I am always drawn to those who need
Rather than want me.
Those who want me I let go.
That's the problem with being an empath;
I can only relate to those who don't see the value in me.
But I'm off track
So let's get back to those in need:
The Blacks, the gays, the immigrants, and true believers in
equality.
Again, why do you fear us, hate us,

Want us once more and for all eternity
Rendered into obscurity?
Why is the world, this world, our world,
Not big enough for you to live next to me?
Why are you terrified to even read about
My histories?
If you're afraid you're in there,
Let me be clear,
We all have the choice to embrace
Or replace any bad memories our
Ancestors shared.
To make new wrongs
Does not make new rights,
Why is that still not clear?!
Being a dick to others
Wont get you hard and into Heaven,
You'll still go limp some year.
You'll stumble into Hell crying
"What went wrong?!"
After God slams their gate
And booms, "YOU DON'T BELONG HERE!
You had your chance, but you refused
To advance the rights of anyone
Who didn't mirror your fears.
That's not what my Son died for.
That not what you say you cry for,
Whenever a new false prophet
Bends your ear. Your fear fills
Your every bone, which is why
You're afraid you'll end alone
If you accept the lives of others
Who share this earth,
but not your political air."

That's it, I've tried.
I've tried not to be cold inside.
I've tried to deflect with love and stay above your righteous,
victimized lair.
But after a while I have to admit
It's not me who has to sit in this.
And the more I address it,
The more I see the mess it is.
And as an empath I have to get clear.
After a breath,
I'll keep trying to wrest
Love, peace, and modernity,
From those who want to return at last,
To a past where I am an invisible memory,
And ban me and mine from books with my history.
So they can feel free.

Black Jobs

I'm about to.
I'm about to run.
I'm about to run out and get me one.
Bout to get me one of them black jobs,
Because I understand I'm supposed to have one.
But I know I got to be quick,
Cause they're not gonna last.
I've been told immigrants are taking them,
And they jump fences fast!
Now, I've heard tee
That there are other ones
Which might be fun to do,
So, they've crossed my mind,
A job or two.
It's in Chocolate City
And there's no walls or fences,
Just some Watergate.
I've heard it's fun,
So I got to run and
Apply for this one.
It's called President of the United States.

Rebuttal

I know you rebut,
I don't get the nut
Of what you think about
People like me, the hip, the woke,
The marginalized communities.
It's not hate, please;
It's my angry black sensitivity
Speaking too loudly!
It's your right to disagree
With everything my kind and I
Live and breathe.
You say this is your freedom debate,
Not a declaration of hate.
We really are sensitive snowflakes.
I retort, well, okay I'll make this short,
Except that I'm loquacious, I snort.
I don't think what you state
represents an innocent difference of
Opinion. I think it smells like
you want to retain dominion.
It's hard to equate collegial debate
With your insistence on deleting my scholastic existence,
Which relegates me and mine to an invisible fate.
Defending the confederacy, is one of your ends;
Is that the lake you want to swim in?
Do you want the South to rise again?
If you find speaking of Black history and Gay rights
To be indoctrination,
I believe the ideology you really seek

Resides in the Aryan Nation.
If you think it right
To deny a child's eyesight
From reading any words
About my authenticity,
Your righteous claim
To be saved in this
salad bowl we both call home,
Is as fake as your religiosity.
You're not brave when you're afraid
To see any words attached to my
Present and past reality.
We obviously know
This land we call home,
You want as a place
Where only you and yours can roam free.
I'm sorry, please pardon me;
I'm back where I started with this soliloquy,
Because your patriotic zeal
Still feels like hate to me.

The Blacker The Berry

I am thrilled
With the Black race
And my black face,
Which is reflected
Everyplace people are seen.

Though it's normally
A variation of brown,
I love that the colors of the
Black race can be found
Wherever the spectrum of
Shades God decreed
Our mortal eyes should be bound.

Black is beautiful.
Its favor is profound.
Explorers coveted cocoa brothers
And chocolate sisters in near and distant towns.
The sweetness of dark berries,
Stripped and sipped,
Has caused generations of hearts to pound.
The denial of African power
Drowns in suckling sounds.

Rebellion

I revile your rebel flag;
It honors rebellion
Against the freedoms
I enjoy.
Breaking foul wind,
It flaps. Sneering,
It chuckles and slaps
Down those who died
For my equality.
You swear it didn't wave
For slavery, but for your
Right to live without tyranny.
But when were your ancestors
Enslaved? What laws were
Required to set them free?

No, the rebel flag flew against
Black equity and signals the same
Today. It bids me go away.
It snarls, threatening me if I stay.
It whips and cracks
"America was greatest when
Blacks had no say!"

When Nazis flash swastikas
Do you believe Jews should
Meekly look away?
Do you deny the tiki torches
Hail Hitler's Third Reich,

Cheering what they thought right,
Eradicating millions who were deceived,
Caged, showered, slain,
All to increase Aryan power
And promote their fascist claim?

You're not blind.
You hate that Blacks are seen.
You feel enslaved by OUR existence.
Today, your banner waves against me.
So, I'll rebel
Against the Rebel Flag's stars and bars
Until my soul escapes their enmity.

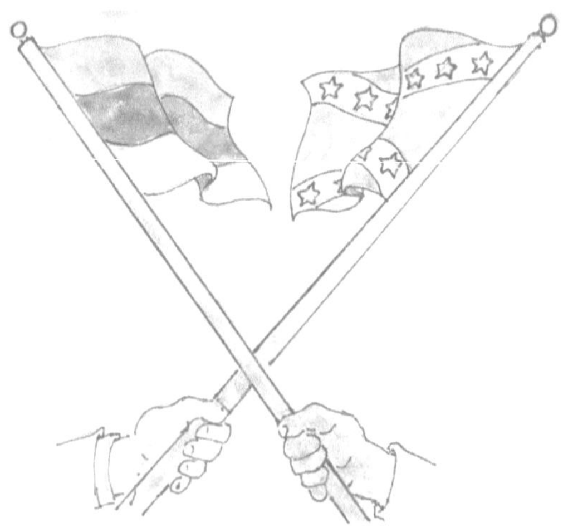

Heroes

Dunbar, Waller, Hughes,
Wilson, Cooke, Gaye,
All heroes who paved the way
For sepia males' artistic immortality.
Oh, so young when I breathed your air
And prayed one day I'd languish there.
Alas, my time seems nearly gone;
Though to cherish you was never wrong.
Until the day I die I'll hail your names
And sing your songs.

Sepia Ariel

For years,
For decades,
For generations
The face of imaginary characters
Was one and the mouse was fine.
Today, imagination has given
Voice to inclusion.
Overnight,
Many poor unfortunate souls
Lost their minds.

Democracy

It is sweet and dense
And delicate and crunchy
Like an ice cream cone.
It is delicious and precious
To hold. It has weight,
Often multiplied and piled on.
We must eat it carefully,
Constantly tasting its constitution.
If we don't, it melts away
And all we're left with
Is a sticky shell.

Blaming the Storyteller

Sorry to wake you,
But now that you are,
I'm not sorry you're awake.
In the past you shouted
Declarations and protestations,
Confident your voice would be heard
Over other's ire, over other's words,
Crowding the victimhood
You ceremoniously owned and served.

While colored mouths were shut out,
You preened the revolutionary clout
You won rebuffing England's crown,
Twelve score and eight years ago
About which you still spangle and shout.
You protest faults you suspect
Rest in the marrow of your bones,
Tainting your righteous claims
For vanquishing the throne.
All in all, considering this historic sprawl,
It seems you'd accept there was good
As well as bad in all human history
And cheer complete stories being told,
But your banner while brave
Is not that bold.

It wasn't about slavery?

Why would a lie
Make you sad?
Why does your chest pound
If you never did anything wrong
And slavery wasn't that bad?

If true,
It makes no sense
To fear children being taught
Facts which are sad.
Heroic blood was shed
Ending the institution
And that should make you glad.
But you cough, gag,
Sputter, spit,
Your disposition dejectedly sags.

The answer to my question
Is different, I guess.

The Line

We're fine.
We're equal.
You defend me
Against conservative chimes.
But when I mention reparations,
Equity draws a line. The years matter.
Your pearls clatter. You check the time.
"I should get money, too. Your folks
Probably had it better than mine."
No longer selfless,
Privilege steps back in.
Fat wallet becomes thin.
When justice dances in moneyed laps,
Black folks
Are liberally left behind.

Snicker

If I slipped you a truth serum
Sweet as a mug of Georgia tea
Spiked with a shot of
Smooth Tennessee Whiskey,
Sipped after a scoop of vanilla ice cream
Melting over a spoonful of hot peach cobbler
Slid down your throat,
And I asked "Why do you
Not want me to vote?"
Would you pat your belly, jerk me close,
Snicker and choke,
"I fear you'd fuck us like slave row,
if y'all had the majority in tow."

Gun Town

What if there was a town
Where all the black folk
Owned guns?
Not just the destitute and the young
(The ones you call thugs and bums),
But the wealthy and the bourgeoisie,
In their town, which they'd run.
Proudly, publicly, openly, they'd carry,
For hunting, and at shooting ranges for fun.
Not political or revolutionary,
But they'd commemorate Tulsa
And vow "Neighbors,
History's history, today's today,
Second Amendment for everyone!"

The Numbers Game

We don't wanna be numbers.
The Tennessee Three.
Central Park Five.
Scottsboro Nine.
Four little black girls blown up.
Three civil rights workers from
Mississippi mud dug up.
Or the first this, the first that,
The first anything
Which shows how long we've been
Down, just as much as it celebrates
That we've stepped up.
Dot's along historical timelines
Don't equate to *Now,*
It's done, aren't you
Satisfied with that?
That's not for me.
Solitary rankings are not
The goal of equality.
When equitable achievements
Are numberless,
Give my numbers a ring.

Racial Man

No one wants to be labeled
Racist,
Despite the laws they pass.
They pledge apple pie days,
So their lies gain a path.
They attract groups they want to please:
Patriot Front; Proud Boys; Aryan Nation;
White Nationalist entities.
But woe if we say
They're bigoted, preachers of supremacy.

Own it,
Embrace it,
You're living it,
Why stammer through
Your grinning mouth?
We're for Black people,
Just not their history.
Excuse me, I'm attending a lecture
On the Lost Cause of the South.

Stop, in the Name of Truth

Stop,
Just stop
Saying that you honor our
Rights,
But hate that we speak
Our nation's truth.

Stop,
Just stop
Saying that you celebrate freedom of
Speech,
But seek to limit the topics
We teach.

Stop,
Please stop
Praising the Jesus
To whom you pray,
But whose teachings you ignore.

Reveal,
Do reveal
What you conceal
When you meet
At dinner tables for meals
To which we are not invited,
Because you're afraid we might share
The anger with which we deal.

You frown that we are around
To remind you of the rights
On which this nation's founded,
On which it's grounded.
During those proud days
When Washington fought,
Jefferson wrote,
And Monroe legislated,
Their enslaved kept their houses warm,
Their families fed,
Belly warmed their guests in bed.

God, ADMIT! Admit
With open eyes, ears, and lips,
We no more fit
Into your American scene
Than we did when our nation's fathers dreamed
And battled the King and British monarchy.
The fathers fought England's taxing their property —
Like their Black Gold,
The enslaved Africans
bound to second class citizenry!

Confess,
CONFESS!
Like Lincoln, Confess,
You're damned if the issue of
Black folk is still your
Goddamned mess.

Pinocchio

I'm angry and Black.
You're racist and White.
I'm tired of these memes,
But if I may be bold,
I'm sick, also,
Of you claiming Dr. King's dream
As your bigot-free code.
You would've hated him,
And Jesus, too - he was poor
and middle eastern,
Lest you forget.
They both wanted the rich
To give to the poor.
You would've seated them,
Side by side, on a boat named
"Liberal Threat."
Tell me that I'm lying,
Tell me their positions
Are those you share.
I'll stand here watching
As your nostrils flare
And your snout grows…

The nose knows,
Pinocchio.

The Color Game

Blue Black
Purple Black
Midnight
Light Bright
Coal Black
Yellow
High Yellow
Redbone
Papersack Tan
Lily White
Tar Baby.
We've had so many names
We've self-claimed. The ones
Others gave us weren't even a
Part of the game. We took the
Pain away by reclaiming the
Shame, dropping bombs on any
Brothers or sisters whose
Blood was stained
With foreign strains.
We knew damn-near-white
Was better than black that
Had to be in the back
Or brown who could hang
Around. Dark was in the field;
Light was in the house.
We laughed and we snarled.
We laid each other out
For being too light

To be Negro and too dark
To be Euro. Slavery labeled
Us in runaway ads and
Sale posts, from tolerably
Black to yellow. We took this
With us when we found freedom's
Road. The purity claim, the
Favored lane, self-hatred infected
Us just the same,
Shaming ourselves
With intra-racist names:
Mulatto, Sambo, Quadroon,
Coon…
Stuck to us like gorilla glue.

Affirmative Actions

I was born in this time
To affirm my being,
To look forward and never back.
I am sworn to raise up those
Who lived before so I might have
Easier days to thrive now.
I proudly mourn my kin
Who didn't live long enough to smile
Because things are better and cry
Because much remains to be done.
One president doesn't balance out
The 43 who preceded him or the two who
Came after. No matter how fly he walked,
Smoothly he spoke, wryly he joked,
Or confidently he owned that
He didn't need to run again,
Because he had "*won them both.*"
I am bound to press on and
Erase this nagging ache over
The hundred, if not thousand
Others who, through proceeding
Generations, were never allowed
To place or show. I affirm that I will
Never cease my efforts to climb
Until laws are no longer necessary
To address, yet another,
Race based crime.

Slap Happy

When you wake up,
I mean
Wake the first fucking time up,
I mean
After the doctor slaps
Your tiny hiney and you howl
Out loud
Up,
With what you don't even
Know is your voice
Up,
You don't know if you're a boy,
Or a girl,
Or perfect,
Or malformed,
Or anything other than what
Your parents have always wanted,
A beautiful newborn baby boo,
Up.

You certainly don't know
That you're Black,
Or White or Asian or whatever
Someone else later tells you,
Or warns you,
Is your pigmentation presentation,
Until a friend or foe wakes you up to it!

You learn to suckle your mother's breast
When you're hungry,

Laugh and coo when you're feeling good,
Cry and scream when you're feeling bad,
And sleep, oh God, sleep,
After you've spent that long ass day
Suckling and laughing and cooing
And crying and screaming,
That's all you know.
That's all you care about.
Until one day you wake up
Again.

This time
YOU WAKE THE FUCK UP
And realize in this world
What you are skin-deep
Is not what matters,
It's the skin people peep
That matters.
That's when your American Dream
Is shattered.

First impression,
First reflection,
First depression.
Depending on how
People see your skin,
How they conceptualize
The skin you're in,
Determines how easily
You can eat, laugh, cry, scream,
Coo, and fall asleep, my friend.
Every day you face that reality
Is like being slapped again.

Black Boy

Black Boys shot for being Black boys.
Black boys gunned down because
They're seen as grown Black men.
Black men targeted as predators
Because they're Black.
Black Men feared as predators,
so little Black boys
Have bullseyes on their backs.

Not just their backs, their bodies.

Grown Black men are treated
Like they're immature little Black boys.
Immature little Black boys are
Shot and killed before
There's any maturing they can do.
They can't grow to be predatory
Or sire future Black kings.

Little Black girls cry
Over their little Black
Brothers, because though
They might outlive them,
They can not defend them or
They may be killed, too.

One World

We are part of a continent
Which formed the world.
We are parts of dynastic
Empires under which innumerable
Banners furled. We are a part
Of this Earth until a presence
Beyond us says we're done.
Why can't we
Harmoniously share
These finite days we have
as one?

Tired

I'm tired
Writing about hatred.
I'm worn
Wailing about bigotry.
I'm exhausted
Explaining why it matters
That we share Black American's
Legacy, because it was hidden
For so long.
I'm positive that this is the
Right path to choose,
But I'm tired of the road.
I'm tired of paving over asphalt
And sidewalks we were afraid
To drive after sundown and
Walk during the day.
I'm tired, but I'll keep marching
So that after I've floated away,
Someone else will rise one
Morning with fresh energy.
I'll be glad I sweated
Tirelessly shedding tears
Over years of racial fears
For my children,
Whom I pray
Will one day say,
"Racism existed? In this country?
Ha! No, fucking way!"

Pepper in your Cream of Wheat

I was that pinch of pepper
In an ocean of Cream of Wheat,
Never fully accepted like
Salt, sugar, butter, or milk.
An exotic herb, touched,
Tasted, swirled, and
Then spat out for bolder
Palates to swallow.
Like seeds in an apple,
My core was seen,
But usually ignored.
I was lonely not being the
Favored flavor, but maybe
That's why I'm still alive
Past the scourge
Of AIDS

Where I shopped

More people liked salt.

Grandma Gave Me a Book

My grandmother gave me a history book.
I thought "Oh lord, one of those." Then I looked.
It had pictures, images of many black faces inside,
I tingled to my toes, a new reality had arrived!
There was Frederick, Harriet, Booker T.,
And George Washington Carver,
The only other hero I knew.
Seeing other faces
Burst my childhood goals beyond just two:
Performing, writing, *and history,*
Became the dreams I'd dedicate my heart and mind to.
Crazy how one little moment
Can place you on a journey
You had no idea you were destined
To pursue.

The author
Class of 1981

Zeona Estelle Eubanks Hatcher Haley
Class of 1923

Everything is Race With You

The minute you open your mouth,
I know what you're gonna slam.
It's Whitey's fault! The system's to blame!
Always the same shit, you claim!
That's why I call you *boy,* I view you as a child
I don't have enough respect to name.

Most servants leave after their chores are done.
So…
Go back to the homes
I stole you from!
Remember, I brought you here?
What made you think
You're the special ones?

I call you black because you're dark.
You call me white because I'm light.
Didn't your poor ass have any crayons
Where you grew up? Shit!
You think color's the reason we fight?
I had guns and you had spears.
I had providence's might.
God's munitions gave me the right.
I'm gonna change that now,
Because the nation's got a conscience?
You're still asleep if that thought
Gives you hope at night.

Do My Ancestors Weep For Me!

Do my ancestors weep for me?
Do they know my name?
Do they rest in peace unaware
There exists a legacy of pain?

Do they question why we remained
In a country which often replaced our
Names?
Do they care we seek comfort
By lifting up their claims?
They can't hear the praise we heap
Upon their unmarked, overworn, graves.

When, as a group,
We chant our forebears' names
And respond to our leader
With shouts of "Ashe!"
Do the forebears smile
Or do they wail,
Having their trauma replayed?

Do they find peace in our libations?
Do they swell with pride over our
Resolve? Or do they wish
With furrowed brows
We'd chase careers over jobs?
Shaking their heads, they say,
"Children, we appreciate you,

But we're gone.
The world's yours now.
Make new memories.
Groove on."

Tearing Down Statues

I tear down your statue
To build up my stature.
You idolize many
Who held me down.

Is it hard to conceive
I'd be reticent to see
Memorials to those who profited
And fought against my humanity?

Do we celebrate busts
Of George III and his royal brain trust
As symbols of American democracy?
I recognize there was a Confederacy,
But in such structures all I see
Are those who fought for the right
To enslave others based on
Racial inequity.

When Did I Know I Was Black?

When did I know there was a difference
Between all the crayons in the box?
It was easy. I opened my eyes,
I Focused. No one had to tell me.
I needed names for the shades and colors,
So I could call out ones I liked best,
The ones I'd want to use the most
And keep near me.

I got a little bit older; and I began to
Notice my shade was rarely on tv.
I knew this because my actor radar
Always scanned for roles I could play.
My ego assured me my time would
Come, my talent would conquer
Scarcity. Whichever future I wanted,
I'd produce with my creativity.
But I noticed the lack.
I realized I was Black when
What was represented was not
My family. People saw people
As crayons, and like my childhood,
Picked the colors they wanted near.
Many people pick the same
Crayons their whole lives. It took
A while for my eyes to appreciate
Darker as well as lighter hues.
But I never thought one
Was better than the other.

Why do you?

Do Better

The wind continues to blow.
The sun continues to shine.
The earth continues to turn.
People continue to love, hate,
Procreate, form families,
Legacies and communities,
Based on similarities, eccentricities,
And commonalities. We build
Cultures and traits which attract
Some and repel others.
This is life. Black and White.
There are so many factors
Over which we can bond or divide.
Using race as the reason is simple.
It's easy. It's cheap.
Look at your neighbor.
Look at the stranger.
Look in the mirror.
Do better.